The Mandatory Daily Cross Life

JOHN K GENDA

© 2021

ISBN: 13: 978-0-9747224-3-6

DEDICATION

To the only wise God our Savior be glory, majesty, dominion, and power, both now and forever. Amen.

FROM THE AUTHOR

This book is not the Bible. I have done my best to bring clarity to some passages with the sincere purpose of drawing us closer to God. The goal is not to show my understanding of scripture, nor that I am the Scriptures' authority. I am not. Although I am afraid to make a mistake, I am still humanly liable to errors. I encourage you to use your Bible and check scriptures to ensure that you don't fall to human errors and that Scriptures are applied for what God wants, rather than what we want.

Let us learn the habits of the Berean Christians in Acts 17:11, who searched scriptures to verify preaching or what they hear: "These were more noble than those in Thessalonica, in that they received the word with all readiness of mind, and searched the scriptures daily, whether those things were so."

May God richly bless you and your family.

John K Genda

THE MANDATORY DAILY CROSS LIFE

What Is the Daily Cross?

Taking the daily cross is one of the most misunderstood concepts within the body of Christ. Christians have attributed the problems, difficulties, hardships, and troubles people experience to their cross. They erroneously say, "That's your cross. You must bear it." Others have believed taking the daily cross means dying daily. They go around saying, "I die daily." We will address these issues as we understand what the daily cross is and how to differentiate between what it is and what it is not.

The Cross of Christ and the Daily Cross

We need to understand the clear distinction between the daily cross and the cross of Christ. The point to note is this: why would Jesus mandate us to take a daily cross if we have been crucified with Christ (Romans 6:6; Galatians 2:20)? Why would Jesus ask us to take the daily cross if He had died once and for all (1 Peter 3:18)? Let us look at what Jesus said about taking the daily cross.

> And He said to them all, If any man
> will come after me, let him deny
> himself, and take up his cross daily,
> and follow me (Luke 9:23).

> And he that taketh not his cross,
> and followeth after me, is not
> worthy of me (Matthew 10:38).

The daily cross is not a piece of a wooden cross that people carry. It is not a physical object but a daily spiritual significance of living for Christ. Daily denying the existence of any form of life in any area of our lives that prevents us from living for the sake of Christ and the kingdom of God is the daily cross. If we listen to the Holy Ghost each day, He will point us to life we have placed in specific areas that need to die through self-denial for the sake of Christ and his kingdom. Each day we wake up, Jesus, through the Holy Ghost, calls us out of life contrary to the life He has given us. We must take the life out of the people and things we have placed life in through daily death, burial, and resurrection so that we can be free and only have the life of God reigning over all areas of our lives. The daily cross is about stopping life that is not the life of God daily. The daily cross is allowing the life of God to reign over any life that aspires to rule over us. The daily cross is the choice to resist, defeat, and put to death the life within human will through the spirit for the sake of Christ and the kingdom of

8

God daily. It is denying human will and accepting God's will in every situation daily throughout our lifetime. Self-denial and daily cross taking is a lifetime duty of a Christian. The daily cross is getting rid of the life of self in areas of our lives in need of the life of God daily. It is about denying the life we have reserved for self in certain areas of our daily living so that God can put His life in those areas through death, burial, and resurrection. The daily cross is Jesus showing us areas in our daily lives where life is not God's will. Jesus knows exactly what is in our life that's not God's will, and that is the life He calls us from daily. Daily life in any area that is not God's will needs death, burial, and resurrection daily. The resistance to self can only be accomplished by faith in what Christ has done for us. If the daily cross is the will of God, then the daily cross is also the resistance and denial of our will. We deny our natural affections for the sake of Christ and His kingdom. Our original Adamic intention is always in resistance to God's will. The daily cross is, therefore, any choice we make in opposition to our will for the fulfillment of God's will. This means putting the life within our will to die daily so that God's life will be resurrected within our will in every situation.

The daily cross is the voluntary choice to execute what personally belongs to us—doing the will of God. This may involve things, people, and places to which our natural affections are tied. This means daily destroying the life we have made out of things or the life we have put in things. The life we put in things must destroyed daily through death, buried and given the life of God again through resurrection. Our education, possessions, status, talents, and everything about us can be given a new life in God's will through resurrection. We can have stuff but our lives in stuff are dead. We can have education, houses, and children, but our life in them can be dead through the cross for God to put the will of his daily life in them. Let us be clear with the word "execution" here; it does not refer to physically killing anyone or any living thing. No human being is worthy to die for the sins of anyone. If anybody decides to physically die on a cross for anyone, such death will be for nothing! Christ died once and for all. No human being is worthy of such sacrifice other than what Christ has done (John 3:16).

In another sense, we can call the cross we are called to bear a daily cross because it is like the death penalty. It is the death penalty to what we have given life to so that that life can be buried and resurrected in God's will and for God. With the daily cross, the legal authority to execute what we own, and our affections for others, is in our hands. We own a will whose life is opposed to God's will, and that's the life we must allow to die on the daily cross each day.

The key is what we lose to honor our Lord. Anything we lose that is not for Christ is not the daily cross. The daily cross has to be for Jesus. It involves denying the natural Adamic will for the sake of Christ—the first Adam for the second Adam; natural life for the supernatural; the old man for the new man; the world for the kingdom of God, and sin for righteousness. This may seem very strange to most Christians today because we have been accustomed to hearing a Gospel without a cross. Many have embraced the strange Gospel of allowing everything and anything to lust without end. The Gospel without the cross is a Gospel of continuous and restless lusting after temporary things and death. I pray at this moment that the body of Christ will open their eyes and understand there is no Gospel or preaching without a cross; hence the importance and inconvenience of the daily cross that expresses what one must lose for Christ and follow God's will. We lose things by taking the life we have placed in them for the life of God's will.

Taking the daily cross is wholly given to choice, not coercion. It is sometimes the death of who we are, what we have become, what we do, and what we own in the fallen Adam. We need to give up our human affections or associations to the fallen Adam in exchange for God's will. It is usually not a pleasant choice because it is based on executing what belongs to self.
What belongs to us in Adam was taken to the cross with Christ, put to death, buried, and resurrected. Every life in Adam must go through death, burial, and resurrection to be sanctified for God. Every area of our life where the life of Adam exist must go to the cross daily so that resurrected life in that area can be experienced. That's the daily work of the Holy Ghost pointing us to the will of God by revealing life that is not of God. I wonder why so many claim to have the Holy Ghost but do not see their daily errors? It varies for each person, because they lose what personally belongs to them for the sake of Christ. As God gives His will to us each day, we must be careful not to resist His will.

Giving up Self to Take the Daily Cross

When we talk about the daily cross, the first thing that comes to mind is the slow and painful death of crucifixion on the cross. "Death" on the daily cross is not instant, and the time to process may vary from person to person. It is usually the slow process to get our lives out of certain things. It takes time for some people to change, and we must be patient with them, just as Jesus was patience with the disciples. With this death comes burial and resurrection into a new life.

The Christian will never experience the joy of the new life without daily executing the presence and authority of Adam. The most pitiful thing is that most Christians do not understand the restlessness and trouble a life without a daily cross brings. A life without a daily cross is a life poured in self and not God.

Taking the daily cross seems like execution because it opposes the Adamic nature and culture and the aggressive will of self. The daily cross can oppose what we have ever achieved, owned, or possessed under the sinful rule of Adam. This does not mean giving up everything you own or have achieved in Adam if God has not told you to do so. God wants you to remove the life you have placed in what you own or have achieved to be placed in Him. Life should be placed in the hands of God, not status or things. This is killing the life of our achievements, have them buried and be resurrected. You are no longer attached to stuff that God has resurrected. Your life is no longer in your education, family, or career, but in God. Those things may still exist, but they are now resurrected without your life in them, because your life in them has been crucified. The cross of Christ has nothing in common to what we were in Adam.

Imagine giving up the person (self) you have known all your life. Self is to whom your mom and dad gave birth. Completely separating the real person you were born as (in Adam) from who you are in Christ can be very painful emotionally because it is separating the created life from birth from the uncreated life from Heaven we receive in Christ.

Sometimes, the cross may require us to let die all we have known, possessed, and worked for all our lives because we achieved it in Adam. This is simply allowing the life we have made out of things to die daily so that we can have things that do not have our life. Everything we do or have must be sanctified for God. This is the reality of the personal daily cross we carry. Although it is not the cross of Christ, it is the likeness of the that cross (Romans 6:4). Failure to let those things die will hinder us from becoming disciples of Christ. With God's help, we should all put ourselves and what personally belongs to us through the process of death, burial, and resurrection. Life outside of God's will must be taken out of our belongings and activities daily so that we can use our lives as God wills.

Biblical examples of those who took or denied their daily cross given to them by Christ include:

- **Abraham**, who resisted his own will to protect his only son. He had to execute his intention to protect his son for the sake of God.
- **David**, who resisted his own desire to stay away from death in order to face Goliath.
- **Saul**, who had the opportunity to put his will to death, but he kept it alive, and the consequences of refusing his cross were the end of his calling.
- **Ananias and Sapphira**, who both had the opportunity of denying themselves, but they chose their own will, leading to their demise.
- **Moses**, who had the chance of being called the son of Pharaoh, but chose God's will so he could lead His people to safety.
- **Joseph**, who was offered free sex, but he chose to deny himself, only to gain more than he could have ever imagined.
- **Achan**, who chose his will over his cross and faced extinction.

Suffering or persecution for any cause other than the sake of Christ or the will of God is not one's cross (Acts 5:41; Hebrews 11:25; 1 Peter 2:20; 1 Peter 4:16; Matthew 10:22; Matthew 5:11). In a fallen world, people suffer continuously for reasons or issues that have nothing to do with the sake of Christ or the will of God. It is wise to avoid telling people what their cross is since the cross does not come from us. No one knows the cross of others. Only Christ knows your cross because it comes from Him.

The Cross Was the Purpose of Christ on Earth

We will get a glimpse of the daily cross by looking at the purpose of Christ on earth: "For I came down from heaven, not to do mine own will, but the will of him that sent me" (John 6:38).

Let us focus on the New Testament daily cross of Jesus before He went to Calvary. Everything Jesus tells us to do, He has conquered successfully and flawlessly. Jesus declared that He came down from Heaven not to live for self, but to do the will of God.

How Jesus came down from Heaven is critical in understanding the cross life of Christ on earth. Jesus did not come down from Heaven through a sexual relationship. If that were the case, then the seed of sinful Adam would have been passed on to Him (Isaiah 7:14, Matthew 1:23). He would have become like Adam in his image.

Since Jesus is divine, He came from Heaven to take up the cross that God gave Him from start to finish. He accomplished this in the incarnation as expressed in John 4:34: "Jesus saith unto them, My meat is to do the will of him that sent me, and to finish his work."

Jesus came to take the cross God gave Him daily up to the end at Calvary that culminates in the atonement for us all. The daily cross Jesus took during His tenure on earth was the absence of self in favor of the presence of God's quickening power. He was God among us and with us. He was the perfect will of using the physical flesh through a virgin paving the way to the absolute will of God for all humanity on Calvary. The daily cross of Christ was a life of obedience to God's will (Hebrews 5:8). It was a pure life without sin because Jesus was the Word in the flesh (John 1:14). He came down from Heaven to take and fulfill a cross.

Jesus in the physical flesh had no relationship to the fallen and death-giving Adam (1 Corinthians 15:45). This means Christ was selfless in taking His daily cross, which was the path to the once-and-for-all cross of humankind at Calvary. God is holy and sinless. Jesus was holy and perfect, because He was God made flesh.

God's holiness is the brightest light that humanity could ever comprehend. The daily cross is exclusively God's will that He gives to us to take or neglect. The cross of Calvary is the will of God given to God in the form of human flesh to pay the penalty for all of humanity's sins and to give believers the power over sin. This cross was given only to Christ, Who came down from Heaven through the conception of the Holy Spirit. God had to become flesh to fulfill His will that no human being born of flesh was worthy and capable of fulfilling.

No one born of flesh would stand a chance of fulfilling the will of the cross given to Christ. Aren't we glad there is no self in the Godhead? Aren't we glad there are no fights of "I will" in the Trinity? Aren't we glad Jesus said, "Father, if thou be willing, remove this cup from me: nevertheless, not my will, but thine, be done" (Luke 22:42)?

The will of God was necessary for fulfilling God's plan of salvation for all those who will accept it, and it is also required of the regenerated Christian to establish God's Kingdom here on earth as we pray (Matthew 6:10-13).

Jesus gives the daily cross to each believer through the Holy Spirit and strengthens us to carry it through the Spirit. At the beginning of His ministry, Jesus invited several people to become disciples. But to become a disciple, one must make the painful choice of putting one's own will to death. This was evident by the response of those Christ invited.

> Then said he unto him, A certain
> man made a great supper, and
> bade many: And sent his servant at
> supper time to say to them that
> were bidden, Come; for all things
> are now ready. And they all with
> one consent began to make excuse.
> The first said unto him, I have
> bought a piece of ground, and I
> must needs go and see it: I pray

thee have me excused. And another said, I have bought five yoke of oxen, and I go to prove them: I pray thee have me excused. And another said, I have married a wife, and therefore I cannot come... And whosoever doth not bear his cross, and come after me, cannot be my disciple (Luke 14:16-20, 27).

And he said unto another, Follow me. But he said, Lord, suffer me first to go and bury my father. Jesus said unto him, Let the dead bury their dead: but go thou and preach the kingdom of God. And another also said, Lord, I will follow thee; but let me first go bid them farewell, which are at home at my house. And Jesus said unto him, No man, having put his hand to the plough, and looking back, is fit for the kingdom of God (Luke 9:59-62).

And as Jesus passed forth from
thence, he saw a man, named
Matthew, sitting at the receipt of
custom: and he saith unto him,
Follow me. And he arose, and
followed him (Matthew 9:9).

And Jesus, walking by the sea of
Galilee, saw two brethren, Simon
called Peter, and Andrew his
brother, casting a net into the sea:
for they were fishers. And he saith
unto them, Follow me, and I will
make you fishers of men. And they
straightway left their nets, and
followed him. And going on from
thence, he saw other two brethren,
James the son of Zebedee, and
John his brother, in a ship with
Zebedee their father, mending their
nets; and he called them. And they
immediately left the ship and their
father, and followed him (Matthew
4:18-22).

And a certain ruler asked him, saying, Good Master, what shall I do to inherit eternal life? And Jesus said unto him, Why callest thou me good? None is good, save one, that is, God. Thou knowest the commandments, Do not commit adultery, Do not kill, Do not steal, Do not bear false witness, Honour thy father and thy mother. And he said, All these have I kept from my youth up. Now when Jesus heard these things, he said unto him, Yet lackest thou one thing: sell all that thou hast, and distribute unto the poor, and thou shalt have treasure in heaven: and come, follow me. And when he heard this, he was very sorrowful: for he was very rich. And when Jesus saw that he was very sorrowful, he said, How hardly shall they that have riches enter into the kingdom of God! For it is easier for a camel to go through a needle's eye, than for a rich man to enter into the kingdom of God. And they that heard it said, Who then can be saved? And he

said, The things which are
impossible with men are possible
with God. Then Peter said, Lo, we
have left all, and followed thee. And
he said unto them, Verily I say unto
you, There is no man that hath left
house, or parents, or brethren, or
wife, or children, for the kingdom of
God's sake, Who shall not receive
manifold more in this present time,
and in the world to come life
everlasting (Luke 18:18-30).

The Daily Cross Comes from Christ

As we can see from the previous Scriptures, the disciples did
not give themselves daily crosses. Jesus gave them daily crosses
because He knew where death needed to take place in each of
our lives. Jesus invited people by calling them from the life
they have created to receive the life He would give them. Some
accepted (like the apostles), while others rejected (like the rich,
young ruler). Even those disciples who took the daily cross
could not carry it because Jesus had not yet ascended into
Heaven (Luke 24:49). Jesus had to help those around Him
carry their daily crosses.

God has been giving daily crosses to people since Adam. He
gave Adam a daily cross, but Adam failed to take it due to the
love of self. Abraham denied his right as a father of an only son;

he died to himself by taking his only son to the place of sacrifice. Paul surrendered his status, position, education in the religious denominational establishment, and all he had to follow Christ. Moses abandoned his status as Pharaoh's son for the sake of God. Jesus gave the Old Testament prophets daily crosses as well, and some failed in taking it, while others succeeded. That is why we always pray for strength to execute the daily cross on earth: "Thy kingdom come, Thy will be done in earth, as it is in heaven" (Matthew 6:10).

God's will is already done in Heaven because there is no self or old man of Adam there. The Adamic nature stops here on earth. No sin enters Heaven. Because of sin and self on earth, God gives us the daily cross to execute His will on earth. Jesus talked about taking the daily cross to His disciples several times and in various ways. In Luke 14:26, Jesus made it clear it is impossible to carry a daily cross with many emotional attachments to and affections toward family and material things. We just read in Luke 18:22 that He gave a daily cross to a young man who became very sorrowful because he was wealthy. The cross here was for the rich, young ruler to sell all he had and follow Jesus. Unfortunately, the rich man did not understand his cross at the time. He knew he had to bury what he had obtained through Adam for Christ to resurrect both him and his substance.

The daily cross is not for unbelievers because it is the will of God. If one has not repented and accepted Christ, then they have no cross to carry. God gives the daily cross through Christ, and one has the choice to either accept or deny taking it. We will all be dead if we are forced to take the daily cross. Self must be crucified with Christ to take the daily cross, which is God's will for each individual. There is a conflict we as Christians face between what we want and what God wants. There are lots of benefits that follow the resurrected life if we can take the daily cross and avoid constant conflict with God. It is impossible to fight the Spirit of the living God and win. The apostle Paul tried it and failed miserably.

You Can't Give Yourself a Cross, But It Will Be Unique for You

Many will wonder and try to use the power of self to determine God's will for their lives. In other words, people will try to give themselves a daily cross that God has not given them and end up in confusion. The will of God, given by God, does not originate from people or self, hence the reason Jesus declared explicitly that we must deny self as a prerequisite for taking on the daily cross.

It is impossible to know and accept the daily cross without being crucified with Christ. The will of God is Christ, which is the life of Christ on earth. A daily cross may not be from God if it is inconsistent with His Word and the life of Christ. It is never God's intention to bring us pain, trouble, persecution, and sorrow to follow Him in fulfilling His will. Although we sometimes may find ourselves in such conditions for our Lord, God wants the best for us at all times. We must put to death by faith anything we inherited from sin to experience resurrection.

We should never wish to have the cross of others. Each cross weighs differently. The things one person may voluntarily lose for Christ and the kingdom of God may not be the things others may suffer. Upon choosing God's will, some will face massive resistance from close relatives; some will lose businesses and established careers; some will receive unfair treatment, and some will deal with physical attacks and even death. Some will be mocked, humiliated, and misunderstood, while some will lose their luxurious lives and comfort. The point here is that whatever is lost for Christ is a cross, no matter how small or big. Some will lose more, less, or all depending on circumstance and Heaven's command.

The daily cross we carry is not the cross of Christ. It is not a team, group, social, corporate, government, or public cross. The daily cross is distinct and personal for each disciple or follower of Christ. The affections of the soul of each are unique in nature, personality, and experience.

What belongs or relates to a particular person may not be the same for another. The state of the soul and personal experiences of individuals are different. Only an individual knows the private aspects of what he or she is or owns in this life that needs execution for Christ's sake. We will never know the matters of another's heart that may require execution. But God is loving enough to show and offer us the opportunity to choose what things need to die in our lives for His sake. There is no formula or compulsion to this. One has to desire God more than self to make such choices.

The daily cross (the will of God) may be different for each person. This was evident in the lives of the Old Testament prophets and the New Testament apostles. What they allowed to die and what they lost for the sake of the gospel were all different. Each prophet or apostle took his daily cross as the Lord gave it to them and carried it in the face of humiliation, disgrace, attacks, abuse, persecution, and sometimes, even death. The same was the story of the saints who followed their God-given paths without hesitation. They lost families and emotional attachments to take the daily will of God. This does not mean they intentionally abandoned families, but rather, families left them. They had the chance to say no to God's will and enjoy the demand of self. They denied self for the will of God.

The cross life points to the selfless servanthood of Christ on earth. It took the disciples a very long time to understand the way of the cross. But once they realized the significance, they weren't afraid or intimidated to willingly give up themselves for the life of the cross. We need the cross life today more than ever because the nature and culture of people are continually changing, but the demands of the cross have not changed. It would not be necessary to carry a daily cross if there is no intention of placing a condemned individual on it. Self life is a condemned life. The fact Jesus emphasized the importance of taking the daily cross indicates we must put to death some form of life. Jesus knows exactly the areas in our lives where we have created self life, and the Holy spirit will point those areas to us daily. We must put the soul life of Adam to death. What has been condemned that we should put to death? This is the question we should be answering. To respond, we must understand death itself.

According to Merriam-Webster's dictionary, death is a permanent cessation of all vital functions of an individual. It is an occasion that causes the loss or the end of life. It is imperative we understand death as it relates to the daily cross. Otherwise, it may lead to confusion or false doctrine.

The cross Jesus mandates us to take is entirely different from the one-time cross of Calvary. The only real (physical) death cross in Christianity was for the payment of the penalty of sin for all, and this is the cross of Christ. No other death on any other cross is accepted for the payment of sin. If one decides to physically die for the payment of his sin or the sins of others, he will die for nothing, and his death would not affect anyone or anything.

The daily cross Jesus is mandating us to take is not for physical death. We are not physically crucified to pay the penalty for anyone, and we do not physically die daily via the daily cross. Scripture made it clear that we have been crucified with Christ (Galatians 2:20). Also, when the apostle Paul talked about dying daily, he was talking about daily risks that can lead to unexpected death anytime during ministry. He was also addressing the doubt of the resurrection of some believers in his dispensation. Understanding what is not death or crucifixion on the daily cross will give us a clear picture of daily self-denial and the execution of the denial.

Now, let us examine what we need to execute daily. The death of Adam as a living soul due to sin resurrected a life of a self-centered soul. Adam's soul was no longer living when he disobeyed God. The authority of the self-life in the soul must cease to exist. The only way we put the directives of the soul life to rest is through self-denial.

The daily cross Jesus was talking about was not referring to the physical death of a Christian. Jesus was demanding the denial of the life of self or the soul life of Adam for a higher life. In other words, salvation is actually denying the life of Adam for the life of Christ. The life of Adam is our natural life, and it seeks to keep us from releasing the authority of self over the soul to the life of Christ. We inherited the life of Adam at birth as our nature, and it remains within us until death.

Talking about the daily cross and self-denial in the body of Christ today is like taking some bitter pills. There has never been a revival in the midst of saints where there is no self-denial. This was evident on the day of Pentecost and on several revivals right here in the U.S.

Are we ready to put the life of our will to death for the sake of God's will?

> And he said to them all, If any man will come after me, let him deny himself, and take up his cross daily, and follow me. For whosoever will save his life shall lose it: but whosoever will lose his life for my

sake, the same shall save it (Luke
9:23-24).

The daily cross basically has two purposes:

A) for the sake of Christ and
B) for the sake of the kingdom of God.

In summary, the daily cross is a life that prioritizes the sake of
Christ and His kingdom over our personal affairs, possessions,
and relationships. The cross links us with Christ and provides
us the sufficiency of life itself. The daily cross takes the life we
have placed in our personal business and puts it to death to be
resurrected as God's will in every business that's pertains to us.

Let us not make false doctrine out of the mandate of the daily
cross by attempting to force crosses on others that God has not
given them. We don't go around looking for crosses to take
without the divine situation or circumstance, either. If God
wants us to give up certain things or relationships for His sake,
He will let us know through His Word, which does not
contradict His holiness. No one should force, coerce, or make
someone guilty in fulfilling their self-interest.

God's people are present in all works of life, and God uses them
as He pleases. Some are doctors, lawyers, judges, engineers,
programmers, technicians, politicians, business people, full-
time ministry leaders, or in many other career fields. If God
wants them to lay aside their careers for Christ, He will let
them know, just as He did with the rich, young ruler, who
rejected the cross. God can use even our careers for the sake of

the kingdom by having them go through death, burial, and resurrection and bringing us to the point where we are willing to count it all loss for His sake. In other words, God takes life out of our careers, talents, status, and achievements through death, burial, and resurrection to give them a new life in His will.

We should never be that ignorant in going around and harassing dedicated Christians to uproot themselves from strategic places God has planted them. Let us allow God to do His work based on what He wants, not what we want. Giving the daily cross is solely the duty of Christ, and when Christ gives the cross, Satan will launch warfare to prevent us from taking it. But Jesus will strengthen us to take it regardless of what Satan does or attempts to do through persecution in our life. All we need to do is to be willing, and God will help us through His Spirit.

Let us be clear that the daily cross as the will of God comes from God through Christ and to each Christian. Christ knows each Christian better than anyone else, and that is why He knows what type of cross each one of us could bear. He knows the capability of each Christian and how they will fit in the body of Christ. He is the only one who knows the areas in our lives where soul life needs to be taken away. Let us pray for strength to be willing to count our lives a loss when it matters for Christ and His kingdom.

A Daily Mandate from Christ

Taking up our daily cross is not optional or discretionary. In the Christian domain, where Christ is the Head, Jesus requires all His followers to carry the daily cross. There is no exception to this requirement under any circumstance. Jesus gives each believer a cross to carry daily. The mandatory daily cross is not a wooden cross, nor is it the cross of Christ. This cross is the daily practice of the will of God through Christ by faith. With the daily cross, believers consider themselves as crucified with Christ daily by faith (Galatians 2:20). The call to take the daily cross is not coercive. It is a call of faith, as it is said in Scripture, that the just shall live by faith (Romans 1:17). In this case, the just is called to live in the victory of Christ every day by the gift of daily faith.

One's status in both the church and the world does not exempt them from the mandate of the daily cross if they abide in Christ (Luke 9:23). Bishops, apostles, evangelists, teachers, preachers, business people, professionals, poor, rich, or any other human distinctions are not exempt. Let me be clear that the choice to follow Christ or accept salvation is never mandatory; it is our free will.

But once an individual follows Christ, then the daily cross becomes mandatory. The mandate to take the daily cross and follow Christ is the same for all who follow Him. This cross is given daily by Christ Himself so that we can walk by faith in the victory He has won for us. We should grow in the good fight of faith, fought by grace to experience the victory of Christ. God has never had a robotic relationship with us by forcing us to choose or serve Him. He freely gives salvation, and the choice to accept or reject His gift is up to us. We are not forced by God to have faith, because faith is a gift of grace.

Jesus opened Luke 9:23 with the conditional statement "if," indicating what He requires of anyone who comes after Him.

> And He said to them all, If any man
> will come after Me, let him deny
> himself, and take up his cross daily,
> and follow me (Luke 9:23).

> And he that taketh not his cross,
> and followeth after me, is not
> worthy of me (Matthew 10:38).

If anyone follows after Him (Christ), then he is expected to accept the conditions of following Jesus as stated in Luke 9:23. Unfortunately, many professing to follow Jesus have not taken the mandate of the cross through faith. Following Christ means giving the rights to our lives over to Him. If we choose to follow

Christ, we should not place our freedoms and rights over His will for our lives. Through Christ, the power of God helps us focus more on the desires and pleasures of God over our passions. Taking the daily cross is identifying with Christ in all areas of our lives each day. It leads us to the place of crucifixion, where self is ultimately put to death by faith in the crucifixion of Christ. We will reach a place by faith, as Paul experienced his crucifixion by daily living through faith in Jesus Christ:

> I am crucified with Christ: nevertheless I live; yet not I, but Christ liveth in me: and the life which I now live in the flesh I live by the faith of the Son of God, who loved me, and gave himself for me (Galatians 2:20)

Jesus wants us to walk by faith daily in the victory He has won for us (John 16:33; 1 John 5:4). We are more than conquerors in God, our Father, Who loves us (Romans 8:37). The Holy Spirit places this love of Christ in our hearts that empowers us to take the daily cross by faith. Our faith in Christ allows the effortless mandate of the daily cross we experience to become a desirous and blessed life. Let us ask God to order our daily steps to understand our limits as Christians in worldly affairs and our cross in kingdom affairs. This understanding leads to a balanced Christian life.

What Is a Mandate?

We can better understand a mandate by looking at real-life examples.

In several organizations or establishments, there are mandatory procedures to follow for those who wish to be part of those organizations. There are also requirements for certain things we need to obtain or status we wish to achieve. Such requirements for organizations or status achievements are not compulsory for all in society, however. These requirements are only for those who wish to be a part of such organizations or achieve such status.

For example, uniforms are not a requirement for everyone in a free society, but if one chooses a profession where uniforms are mandatory for everyone, then he or she is required to wear that uniform. The desire to drive a vehicle is never mandatory, compulsory, or binding on anyone, but if anyone chooses to drive, then obtaining a license and car insurance becomes mandatory. It is out of desire or free will that we make the choice. Just as salvation is not compulsory or mandatory, so is the choice to drive. Board certifications are not mandatory or binding on any citizen in a free society, but if a person desires a specific professional practice, then board certifications for such practices are required. The cross is not mandatory for those who have not decided to follow Christ.

People are called to mandatory actions because laws or rules require them to do so. In our natural world, there are penalties for violating laws. Most of the time, natural mandates are not applied with grace and mercy. Let us put Christ's mandate in perspective before moving further with discussing the cross life.

The sole purpose and intent of Christ's mandate is for our benefit in our walk with Him. Obeying this mandate of faith improves our lives, families, and societies. We cannot compare it to the merciless laws of men that result in swift judgment. Paul, in the book of Romans, conveyed a balance of grace and law so there would be no confusion in pursuing the mandate of the cross. It is for those who choose to follow Christ.

Christ said, "If any man will come after me" (Luke 9:23), meaning He has created the path to the finish line. We need to use the same faith we used to accept the gift of grace to also accept the mandate of the cross life. Jesus wants us to understand that He has won the victory for our lives. This mandate of the daily cross life is a mandate for daily victorious living through Christ.

Who Can Follow Christ and Receive His Mandate?

Let me be clear about salvation. Salvation is only by God's grace and has nothing to do with us (Ephesians 2:8-9). This faith to live the victorious life through Christ is a gift through His finished work. God does not require our human ability or effort to provide His grace. Salvation is the work of God and is free for all who accept and believe in Jesus. It is for everyone, everywhere, and it is up to each one of us to either accept or take this gift, or we can choose to reject or abandon it.

But once we accept the gift of salvation, then taking the daily cross becomes mandatory. It is through this mandate that we experience the gift of salvation. It is virtually impossible to understand the daily cross without understanding the once-and-for-all-finished cross of Christ. To take the daily cross, one must be linked to the finished cross of Christ (John 19:28-30).

The effect of teaching about taking the cross daily in our family devotion at home truly blessed my heart. The day after teaching about the cross, my six-year-old surprised me when I came home from work.

She handed me an envelope and said: "This is for you. Open it."

When I opened the envelope, there was a paper cross she had made.

She said, "I made a cross for you because the Bible says everyone must carry a cross."

I also noticed she had made paper crosses for her mom and siblings as well. Her understanding of the cross showed me how much work is needed to help her comprehend the fact that the daily cross we carry is not a physical one, and it is also not the cross of Christ. One takeaway from the lesson was that she grasped the importance of taking the cross daily and wanted each family member to have a cross to carry.

If anyone follows Jesus, then taking the daily cross becomes a requirement:

> For whosoever will save his life shall lose it: but whosoever will lose his life for my sake, the same shall save it ... For whosoever shall be ashamed of Me and of My words, of him shall the Son of man be ashamed, when he shall come in His own glory, and in his Father's, and of the holy angels (Luke 9:24, 26).

It is about time for the church to understand that taking up the daily cross is mandatory and not an option, and it means implementing what Christ finished on Calvary. Refusing to carry our daily cross is refusing to follow Christ. It is impossible to follow Christ and leave the daily cross behind (Luke 9:23) because then, we are only following ourselves.

The mandate of the cross hasn't changed at all. Through the cross of Christ, Jesus paid for our sins, and the Spirit empowers us to take and carry the daily cross. It is of great importance to understand there is no Christianity without a cross. The daily cross reflects the life we are expected to live as Christians. The daily cross distinguishes the image and likeness of Adam from the new birth in Christ.

Accepting the Mandate of the Daily Cross

Those who have accepted this mandate are experiencing the best life that can only come from above. God is not a respecter of persons, and He can do the same thing for those willing to accept the requirements of the daily cross (Romans 2:11), which gives meaning and appreciation to life.

Because Christ loves us so much, He wants us to experience a life of victory, even as the enemy's forces confront us daily. He has defeated Satan and his demons through the cross, and He gives each Christian a daily cross for the daily battle of maintaining a victory He has already won. "Who is he that overcometh the world, but he that believeth that Jesus is the Son of God?" (1 John 5:5).

On the whole, Christ's command is to accept what He has done for us by living for His sake and the kingdom of God. The mandate of the cross emanates from God's love and care toward us. That is why the cross is never a requirement until we follow Christ. Once we decide, then we should deny our natural life daily for the sake of the new life from Heaven. It is never God's desire for His children to lead a double life.

The natural life of Adam in which we were born is conflicting to being born again with a new life from Heaven. Jesus wants our real life to be the life of the cross and not the life of Adam. Satan is very crafty in using the natural life of Adam, so we can live for his sake and his worldly kingdom.

37

Christ, on the other hand, wants us to live for His sake and the sake of God's Kingdom. As soon as we follow Christ, a lifetime of warfare is initiated as Satan, who wants nothing more than to be the sole ruler of our natural life, refuses to give up authority to our new life from Heaven. The purpose of this conflict is that Satan never wants us to do what God wants, and he will settle for a double life from us instead.

Christ does not settle for a double life from us, however. He commands us to get into a conflict of denying what we want for the sake of what God wants by taking the mandate of the daily cross. The fight is on until we die, but Christ empowers us to stay in the war of maintaining the victory in the cross.

The mandate of the cross of Jesus Christ makes the life of daily warfare simple, understandable, enjoyable, and glorious for those who accept it.

Fulfilled and Unfulfilled Cross

There is a powerful correlation between the fulfilled cross and the unfulfilled cross. The fulfilled cross is the cross of Jesus on Calvary, and the unfulfilled cross is our daily cross. The power to take and carry the daily cross comes from the fulfilled cross of Christ (Philippians 3:10). It is okay to keep telling people to live holy, but we must also inform them that the power source for holy living comes from the fulfilled cross of Jesus Christ (Hebrews 10:10).

The Father gave the Son a cross, and the Son fulfilled the cross perfectly, hence the reason Christians can refer to the cross of Christ as the finished cross: "it is finished" (John 19:28-30). Jesus, the only begotten Son of God, was the only One worthy of fulfilling the cross given by the Father. No human being born of flesh was worthy enough to fulfill the cross given by the Father. The cross of Jesus Christ is the atonement for the sins of the entire world. It is a once-and-for-all cross. It is not a daily cross. The death of Christ was not for any other reason but for atonement for the sins of the whole world (Leviticus 17:11; 1 Peter 2:24; 1 John 2:2; Romans 5:6-11; Hebrews 9:12).

God exalted the Son to have all powers in Heaven and on earth (Matthew 28:18-19), and all control in both of these realms belongs to Christ. He holds the keys to death and hell. Everything both in Heaven and on earth goes through Christ. We need God's power to flow from the cross of Christ to our daily cross. The fulfilled cross is a finished cross. It was for Christ and Christ alone (Hebrews 10:5). It does not refer to the cross we are told to take daily because Jesus declared, "It is finished: and he bowed his head, and gave up the ghost" (John 19:30).

We Can Take the Daily Cross Because of the Fulfilled Cross

The Master of the completed cross gives the daily cross, and we must take it daily if we will become useful Christians. We must render our own selves powerless for the rulership of Christ. Self must be subject to the principles of Christ.

The finished cross is the will of God given to Christ, while the unfinished cross is the daily will of God given to each believer by Christ. We must take and fulfill the daily cross given by Christ the best we can. Most of us get to the point of taking the daily cross but are too weak to carry it. We have too much stuff of self in our hands and no place for the cross at all. We cannot take the daily cross together with self. We should never permit self in the realm of following Christ.

The fulfilled cross is like a transmitter of God's will, while the daily cross is like the receiver. We experience constant

40

transmitting and receiving of God's will in the realm of the cross.

It is very important to understand the correlation between the continuous personal daily cross and the once-and-for-all-completed cross of Christ. There needs to be a spiritual connection for us to experience the finished work of Christ. The once-and-for-all-completed cross of Christ was given to Christ by God the Father for payment of the penalty of our sins and for giving us power over sin. Christ gives us daily cross for us to experience power over sin. Since the daily cross comes from Christ Himself, then we can say it is in the likeness of His completed cross (Romans 6:3-5).

There is a spiritual connection between our daily cross and the cross of Christ. Christ emphasized this connection on the continuity of the daily cross until our physical death. All powers in Heaven and on earth have been given to Christ. Staying connected to Christ, Who has power over sin, enables us to experience victory over sin. Christ provides the ability for each child of God to experience this conquering of sin. In other words, we can't experience the new life outside the cross territory. Experiencing the daily cross is living in the power and glory of God.

Satan fights against the daily cross aggressively because he does not want the believer to abide in Christ (John 15:4-6). Satan knows if the believer abides in Christ, he has no chance over him. Making progress in the Christian walk is contingent on the daily cross becoming a priority. We must strive to go forward with the cross and go after the fulfilled cross intentionally.

God Teaches Us through the Cross

The fulfilled cross is where God reveals the peculiarity of our identities, shows us who we are, and teaches us the difference between a godly person and a worldly person. He teaches everyone from the spirit and soul, as well as to the body (1 Thessalonians 5:23).

The dealings of God lead to a very humbling experience. The process involved in surrendering self to death can be painful; this is where complete deliverance from lust, pride, and other sins takes place. The will of the soul is transformed to obey God's will. As growth in God's presence takes place, and sin is dealt with from the inside, a transformation from inside out happens (Philippians 2:12-13). It is not a metamorphosis from the outer man to the inner man. In other words, we are restored to the correct order of operations.

As we live for God, His Spirit is now in charge of our souls, and it communicates to our spirits ways we can discern attributes of God and His plan. Our spirit instructs our soul, and our soul sends information for our physical senses to execute (1 Corinthians 2:11). This order of operations is quite different from what we inherited from Adam, where the authority of self initiates everything in the soul.

Christ accomplished and finished the cross once and for all. The daily cross that Christ requires of us is permanent until we die. This explains the difference between an all-powerful God and man's limitations. God does not need a daily cross, but we do.

The cross of Christ and the daily cross are not the same. The cross of Christ paid the penalty for our sins and gave us power over sin once and for all. Our daily cross derives power from the cross of Christ to serve a great purpose. We should all seek to know the purpose of our daily cross.

The daily cross is not something any single individual can master. That is why we have to take it daily until death. If we can master the daily cross with human strength, then Christianity would be nothing but an institution where one would graduate in taking the daily cross. No Christian is immune to failure or trouble; we are all vulnerable to life's challenges, hence the need to take a daily cross empowered by the finished cross of Christ. As we rely on the finished work of Christ, we realize the possibility of successfully taking the daily cross.

The connection between the daily cross and the completed cross of Christ should improve continually and without gaps. Successfully taking the daily cross depends on our relationship with Christ.

The body of a Christian on earth is the temple of God. The power that runs this temple comes from the Father through

Christ to us. God never runs out of power, but to experience His power, we need to link to Christ: "And, behold, I send the promise of my Father upon you: but tarry ye in the city of Jerusalem, until ye be endued with power from on high" (Luke 24:49).

We must maintain our link to Christ with the help of the Holy Spirit so that we can continue to experience God's power until physical death. The power from the fulfilled cross is available to us for carrying the daily cross, and there is enough available for our entire lifetime on earth. It flows continuously from the Father through the fulfilled cross of Christ onto our daily cross.

The Cross Territory

One place where Satan has no access and doesn't want us to be is the daily cross territory. Satan will fight so hard to get us out of it because inside is the journey of following Jesus after self-denial. It is the territory where God strengthens us to carry His will daily and overcome the world continuously. We've got to step into God's territory for us to accept His will and carry it because it launches every effective activity of a Christian.

A New Journey to Follow Christ

We step into the cross territory when we abandon self and take the cross to follow Jesus. It is the journey a believer takes to be one with Christ. This goal of taking the daily cross is to close the distance between Christ and us so that we can become one with Him (John 17:21). It is not Christ's intention to have a gap between Him and us as we follow Him. Our willingness to deny self determines how close or far we are from Christ. Christ wants no separation to exist between us and Him. He wants us to abide in Him (John 15:4).

The goal of Christ is not only for us to follow Him, but to have direct access and contact with Him (John 1:12). The closer the believer gets to Christ, the more they experience resurrection power (John 15:7) because they hear and see things in the spirit realm hidden to the public (1 Corinthians 2:11).

Life begins a new phase in new territory when we deny self its authority and follow Jesus. We enter a new territory where we close all doors to the devil. Satan has no means to trigger or influence the soul without self; instead, he depends on self to work one hundred percent. We can only launch life in the new cross territory after self-denial. Each day, Satan attempts to stop us from entering the territory of the cross and experiencing the life of Christ.

Outside of the cross territory is where the devil has access to the soul. We cannot deny self outside the cross territory. The devil comes and goes as he pleases through self. If we do not take the daily cross, then there is no barrier between the devil and the soul.

The cross territory is walking in the way Jesus has created. It is not a way created by mind games or intellectual prowess that appeals to us. It is a personal walk for each follower of Christ that closes all access to the devil. The devil has no access to those in the cross territory; he may cause physical harm or disturbance to them, but he can't touch or confuse their souls. As the believer locks the doors to self, he lives between the daily cross and the cross of Christ. As the believer lives in Christ, the devil has no way of winning a fight against

Christians because the devil sees Christ and not the believer
(John 15:7). The grace that flows from the finished cross covers
believers in the cross territory. Operating within the perimeter
of the cross continually keeps the devil at bay.

We should deny self and leave it outside the cross territory. The
territory of following Christ does not need self or personal
belongings. The only need present is the daily cross. We should
not take this to the extreme by jumping to the conclusion that
there is no need for personal belongings. We should deal with
what we own or accomplish based on the sake of Christ and the
kingdom of God. This is not implying we get rid of life's
necessities when not sanctioned by God.

Whatever we do has to be for Christ's sake. When a saint is
moving in the territory of the cross after Jesus, he has no time
for what goes on around him outside the cross territory. He
dwells there and victoriously defeats the devil, with Christ at
the lead of warfare. Christ Himself has walked this path; we
just need to follow with the daily cross.

The cross is the only vehicle that takes us through the journey
of life and into the territory Jesus has given us. Christ formed
the precedent of how we should carry the cross. The daily cross
we carry has no global destination as long as we are alive. It is a
lifetime journey.

God's Power Fuels Us

The cross territory is where the difference between heavy, exhausting religious practices and burdens that have nothing to do with Christ are crucified. His yoke is easy, and his burden is light (Matthew 11:28-30). Satan's lies are exposed, and we accept revelations about God's ways. We begin to see the fulfillment of God's Word in all the affairs of humanity. We move from emotions of the soul to emotions of the Spirit, and we begin to understand issues as God sees them.

In the cross territory, God deals with us based on the process of time. The life of the cross is never based on our time. God guides us and everything concerning us so that we can operate and live in His image and likeness. As long as we have accepted Christ and the will of the cross, we should never be anxious about when, why, and how. We go to God in communion through prayer and fasting and ask Him to open our spiritual eyes and ears to see what the world can't see and hear in every situation.

In the cross territory, praise, worship, and ministry are no longer on our terms. When we follow Christ, we submit the operation of our entire being from head to toe to His direction. This type of life goes beyond the soul as we submit the soul to divine order.

Although natural Christians may not understand waiting on God for leading and guidance, those in the cross territory understand the significance because they are not living for themselves. They are living the life of the continuous, daily cross fueled by the power of the finished cross. They spend much time on spiritual things, such as prayer, fasting, and benevolence. They are united with Christ via the channel between their daily cross and the finished cross of Christ. They rely on the spiritual principle that to hear from God, they must connect to Christ because He tells only what He hears from the Father (John 16:13).

The devil has no chance over a soul in a divine territory who operates on divine orders. This is why Satan doesn't want the saints to understand and take the daily cross. Serving God outside the cross doesn't bother the devil because there is still a way for him to access our souls. Satan is angered if he can't control us at will because he understands a Christian's importance and effectiveness in the cross territory.

The Christian in the cross territory can revive others. A person whose spirit has been empowered through Christ can touch the spirit of others. This real revival comes through those who accept and take the daily cross to preach the finished and completed cross of Christ (1 Corinthians 1:18-20). How can we preach the cross of Christ if we have not taken the daily cross? God provides us with great balance and stability in the cross territory in His time (Proverbs 16:11). For example, I had the opportunity to teach our just-turned-sixteen-year-old daughter how to drive. The scariest thing is that she either goes too slow or too fast. This makes my heart jump up and down. After a few lessons, she surprised me with some stability behind the wheel. This is how our walk with God sometimes is: we either go too fast or too slow until God brings us to a stable walk alongside Him. I pray God will bring those of us going too fast ahead or too slow behind into a stable stride with Him.

If we fail to ban ourselves from self, we will never enter the cross realm and experience divine life. This is a realm where self is prohibited. Jesus made it clear that we can't bring self along if we want to follow Him. This means that if we are not willing for God to deal with self, we can't follow. Let us spend more time on dealing with ourselves so that we can take the cross and allow God to deal with us. We should be willing to go before God and ask Him to do a work in us and avoid wasting time in investigating what He should do in others.

Seeking Repentance to Find Righteousness

God gives us a clear conscience about every issue or circumstance we face in the cross territory when we seek sincere repentance. We are truly and sincerely able to repent of our sins and experience the sanctification of God in the territory of the cross. Repentance in the cross territory is accepting the death sentence of self and delivering it to the cross for crucifixion. Most of us in the church have not truly repented, and that is why we are still alive in the old ways of man and living confused double lives (Matthew 6:24). The process of Christianity required of all who choose to follow Christ is death, burial, and resurrection. We must die to follow. Lord, help us to die to self. How painful it is!

It is only in the cross territory that we can realize the destructive and damaging nature of sin. Sin can render us spiritually braindead to keep us ignorant of its destructive practices within us.

When Jesus opens our eyes, it is like *Wow!* This thing called sin is a slow killer. The opening of our eyes helps us know how sin was destroying us (Matthew 4:16-18). When we take the cross, Jesus will not only show us what sin has done to us, but he will also heal us (Isaiah 53:5).

We will never confess our worthlessness or uselessness without being humbled by grace. A Christian's pride is ungodly and usually a result of self. There is no such thing as "super" spirituality or "super" righteousness in the cross territory (Isaiah 53:5). We are humbled as God shows us our mess, and He empowers us to fight daily in pursuing righteousness and sanctification.

Lord, help us to be humble and depend on You for all things and at all times (1 Peter 5:6-7). Deliver us from the useless and hopeless pride of self.

The daily cross constantly reminds us of humility, and we find our complete freedom in the cross territory. We should depend on God for everything and boast not about our capabilities today or tomorrow: "For that ye ought to say, If the Lord will, we shall live, and do this, or that" (James 4:15).

We should live within the entire territory between our cross from the point of following Christ to the victorious completed cross of Christ. The faith we experience at the cross territory far exceeds the faith for what we want (Hebrews 11:6). It is the faith to live a life God wants whether we profit from it or not. The Christian life is more of a fellowship than a business.

I pray that our desire goes past just being in the cross territory to actually touching Jesus Christ so that we can have a vine-and-branch relationship (John 15:5). Christ as the vine continually supplies support to us, the branches, throughout our lifetime here on earth so that we stay healthy and alive. We need to be within the cross territory to take dominion. Outside the cross territory, we will have no dominion over the devil. Joshua 1:9 should remind us today that God has given us the authority to take territories of the devil and convert them to cross territory with Christ leading us.

Lord, help us understand and empower us to take the daily cross.

The Cross Life Is Based on What Christ Has Done

The path of the daily cross is not one mankind can create because no human being is worthy to create it. This path is not something that corporations, institutions, or religions could invent. Even the best Bible school in the world can never manufacture the path of the cross.

The Lamb of God, Who became flesh and dwelt among us, created the path (Revelation 1:18). Following Jesus has nothing to do with the methods and paths humanity created but is all about the Way, the Truth, and the Life (John 14:6).

God has given us His plan to follow. We can't make our own plan and invite God to follow it. No human can force God into submission to human will, although many try ignorantly. The ways of God have become a huge business empire, as many have developed self-ideas about getting things from God, hearing from God, and thus and thus. Who can think of God as to direct Him (1 Corinthians 2:16)? Can a human being or a living soul manage God?

> For what man knoweth the things of a man, save the spirit of man which is in him? Even so the things of God knoweth no man, but the Spirit of God...For who hath known the mind of the Lord, that he may instruct him? But we have the mind of Christ (1 Corinthians 2:11, 16).

The daily cross life is implementing what Christ has done. Our redemption, deliverance, sanctification, faith, holiness, and warfare are because of what Christ has done, and we base our entire Christian faith on all of that. It is a false doctrine to come up with methods and steps outside the cross to experience Christ's work. We must pass through the cross to experience what Christ has done and secured for us.

The intellectual and emotional life of Adam has nothing to do with what Christ has done. Christ has laid down the path of the cross for us to follow. To walk in the path Christ has established, we must deny ourselves and take up the cross daily.

We cannot accomplish taking the cross and following Christ by our human might and strength (Romans 8:13). It is a complete spiritual walk of the soul manifested in experience. Human might alone has no power over the human soul.

Faith is Understanding Christ's Work

Faith activates the new life in Christ, and we need faith to maintain it. Faith not only stops at salvation, but it should also continue throughout a Christian's life. The Scripture did not command us to come to Jesus and let Him follow the ways of the old man; it commands us to come to Jesus and follow Him. Since we are powerless over self, we need to offer self on the cross daily and let the cross handle it.

> For whatsoever is born of God overcometh the world: and this is the victory that overcometh the world, even our faith. Who is he that overcometh the world, but he that believeth that Jesus is the Son of God? (1 John 5:4-5).

> Jesus saith unto him, I am the way, the truth, and the life: no man cometh unto the Father, but by me (John 14:6).

> Ye have not chosen me, but I have chosen you, and ordained you, that ye should go and bring forth fruit, and that your fruit should remain:

55

that whatsoever ye shall ask of the
Father in my name, he may give it
you (John 15:16).

Jesus said unto her, I am the
resurrection, and the life: he that
believeth in me, though he were
dead, yet shall he live: And
whosoever liveth and believeth in
me shall never die. Believest thou
this? (John 11:25-26)

I am Alpha and Omega, the
beginning and the ending, saith the
Lord, which is, and which was, and
which is to come, the Almighty
(Revelation 1:8).

The LORD shall cause thine enemies
that rise up against thee to be
smitten before thy face: they shall
come out against thee one way, and
flee before thee seven ways
(Deuteronomy 28:7).

Behold, I give unto you power to
tread on serpents and scorpions,
and over all the power of the
enemy: and nothing shall by any
means hurt you (Luke 10:19).

Verily I say unto you, Whatsoever
ye shall bind on earth shall be
bound in heaven: and whatsoever
ye shall loose on earth shall be
loosed in heaven. Again I say unto
you, That if two of you shall agree
on earth as touching anything that
they shall ask, it shall be done for
them of my Father which is in
heaven. For where two or three are
gathered together in my name,
there am I in the midst of them
(Matthew 18:18-20).

No human being is capable of being the resurrected sacrifice.
No man can die and self-resurrect. The purpose of taking the
daily cross is not to repeat what Christ has done and
accomplished. Such accomplishments are exclusive to divinity
only. Our role in the cross walk is to believe Jesus is the Son of

God, God the Father, and the Holy Spirit, because He is capable of resurrecting Himself. Our life flows out of the belief that Jesus is the Life and the Resurrection. This belief activates a faith that connects us to the path we should follow through the daily cross.

We do not choose what we want to lose for Christ; rather, He tells us what he wants us to lay aside for Him, hence the painful separation on our part. Through the Spirit, Jesus lays down the path for each Christian to follow. When Jesus lays the path for us, we must be willing to accept and follow it. It can be a struggle if we do not like the path Jesus give us, but we need to pray with agony until self leaves, and the power of grace enters. Lord, give us the grace to pray so that we can be strengthened to say, "Lord, not my will, but Your will be done."

I may not like the path, but God, help me to accept it.

Practicing the Daily Cross Through Daily Communion

Applying the Holy Communion concept as a practice in taking the daily cross would be incredibly beneficial in our growth as Christians. Communion creates an environment for us to be sensitive to the work of the Holy Spirt. The Holy Spirit brings the effect of the cross of Christ into one's life by transferring divine work to the human experience. Our daily life should be a life of communion with Christ (1 Corinthians 11:24-25).

Fellowship with Jesus within us should become natural to us. It is through communion that Christ gives us the daily cross for God's will. We should avoid every obstacle that prevents our daily communion with Christ within us. The intimate time of worship in daily communion does affect our hearts and outward conduct. The Spirit of communion should be kept alive within us by continuously remembering what Jesus has done for us and sharing it with others. Communion is a fresh reminder of how the supernatural work of Christ in establishing the new covenant affects our physical life. Communing with Jesus from within enables us to learn from Him. Jesus not only comforts us, but He also teaches us and corrects our errors inwardly. The communion with Jesus through the Holy Spirit affects the nature of our souls, which determines our actions.

According to the Oxford dictionary, communion is the sharing or exchanging of intimate thoughts and feelings, especially when the exchange is on a mental or spiritual level.

Bringing the idea of daily communion to our daily lives does not mean that we should abandon communion with our brothers and sisters in Christ or breaking bread from house to house. Daily communion with Christ within us Christians should never replace the communion of believers together to use bread and drink to remember the death of Christ and the new covenant for all humanity. No human activity should replace the remembrance of the substitutionary death of Christ for us. The sharing and exchanging of our intimate thoughts and feelings with Christ should not be interrupted by any event, because it is internal.

This concept of communion can even apply to our daily lives. For example, if there is no holy, intimate connection in feelings and thoughts with our children or spouses, then we have broken relationships. That is why Satan tries his best to pull us towards intimate connection in thoughts and feelings with electronic devices so that we can have a broken relationship with those who matter to us.

Christ, through the Holy Spirit, is part of our lives, and we need to have intimate relationships with Him. Daily communion with Christ from within keeps us connected with Him. We should do our part to ensure that we stay connected through the works of faith. Christ should be on our minds daily and always. If our nature has not been trained to do so, then we must set daily alarms to train our nature for intimacy in thoughts and feelings for Christ. Human nature can be trained by faith through the spirit to do the things of God. Our addictions to electronic devices are a proof that humans can train themselves to crave and have intimacy for God, so instead of relying solely on social media, let us learn to talk to Christ in our thoughts when we are idle.

Although the Bible does not state the frequency of when we should take holy communion, we are instructed by Christ to have communion as often as possible until the Lord returns. We can take this concept of communion with believers, apply it to our daily lives, and have communion always.

Let us imagine how valuable it would be in having communion with Christ in our thoughts, minds, souls. We can't be in sin and commune with Christ. We must repent before we enter such sweet communion. Whether we think we are righteous or holy, we must still repent in approaching a holy God. Participation in daily communion is never a sinful manner;

hence, we only hurt ourselves spiritually when we are in sin. We need to repent daily to have fellowship with Christ, and the power of His blood will give us control over sin. Therefore, the first step in this daily communion is repentance.

Regular or daily communion with Christ will deliver us from self-centeredness, sects, factions, class distinction, political cliques, and any other form of division.

Christ has complete control. Spiritual power over human nature, as well as the power to bring the sinful human nature to subjection, comes from Christ. God is too holy to deal with us directly. If He does, His holiness will kill us, so He communicates with us through His intercession of Christ, Who gives us the Holy Spirit.

How we relate to the body of Christ affects how God relates to us. If we can keep communion with Jesus uninterrupted, our daily actions will come from our communion with Christ. Our actions will come out of service and love for others. Our actions will be like Christ because of communion. Daily communion with Christ will prevent us from ungodly communion with Satan and help us avoid demonic influence.

Most of us have heard the saying "What would Jesus do?" If we are always in communion with Jesus, there is no need to ask the question, because He will tell us exactly what to do through the power of the Holy Spirit. In communion, Jesus is in charge. If we listen to Jesus in communion, we will know what to say, hear, and do.

In communion–specifically, His last supper–Jesus Himself broke bread and passed the cup. The bread symbolized His body (the lamb of God), and the cup of wine symbolized His blood (New Covenant). Communion with Christ involves eating, drinking, thanksgiving, sacrifice, and a covenant.

Eating and drinking are daily activities of living beings. We eat and drink continuously under normal circumstances. If we do not do these things for a prolonged period, we get tired, eventually getting sick.

The new man created after righteousness needs to eat spiritual food and drink spiritual drink for us to grow (Ephesians 4:24). Spiritual eating and drinking have to be done daily without interruption. We have to remember that Jesus Himself said "My food, is to do the will of him who sent me and to finish his work" (John 4:34).

Jesus Himself presided over communion; therefore, in communion, Jesus directs our lives through the sacrifice of His body and covenant for us. We learn how to use our bodies as living sacrifices because we have a new covenant with God. As it is said: "I beseech you therefore, brethren, by the mercies of God, that ye present your bodies a living sacrifice, holy, acceptable unto God, which is your reasonable service" (Romans 12:1).

As stated earlier, though the Bible did not state the frequency of taking holy communion, Jesus instructs us to have

communion as often as possible until the Lord returns.
Applying the Holy Communion concept as a practice in taking
the daily cross is incredibly beneficial in our growth as
Christians. Let us imagine how valuable it would be to have
communion with Christ in our thoughts, minds, and souls.
Communion with Jesus in our souls will determine our actions.

> But those things which proceed out
> of the mouth come forth from the
> heart; and they defile the man
> (Matthew 15:18).

We should remember two crucial things in eating and drinking
when it comes to daily communion: the bread representing
Christ's body and the drink representing His blood and the new
covenant.

Apart from the covenant with God and man, the other lifetime
covenant we see similar to communion is marriage. In
marriage, two become one, while in communion, we become
one with Christ. Oneness with Christ far exceeds any other
oneness in this life and in the life to come. We should practice
the daily remembrance of communion until the concept
becomes real in our lives.

When we wake up in the morning, our daily routines seem
natural. We wake up, wash up, and look for food. Communion
becomes palpable when we treat it like daily hygiene and a
necessity.

The remembrance part of communion should be daily. Remembering here is very important. To remember simply means bringing the past into present thought and feelings. It is easy for us to forget the purpose of Christ on earth if we can't remember His communion. We should have the same daily desire we have for eating and drinking for communion with Christ. We should hunger and thirst after Christ daily. When we hunger and thirst, we must eat the bread He provides and imbibe the drink He gives (John 6:54-58). I hope this is understood in the spiritual context so that folks don't sit around waiting for Christ to offer them a physical bread and drink.

As we practice daily communion with God, we will begin to be conscious of the specific routines required for a healthy, daily Christian living. This consciousness leads to daily practice until it becomes a habit, like eating and drinking. Jesus does not want us to see the Christian life as an on-and-off event. We should not confine the Christian life to a church program or get-together; rather, it should be drawing strength from what Christ finished. A new life does not mean on-and-off of life and death, either. It is continuous.

As Jesus Himself said: "And he said to them all, If any man will come after me, let him deny himself, and take up his cross daily, and follow me" (Luke 9.23). From the aforementioned passage, Jesus wants us to take the cross daily, meaning continuously without interruption.

Jesus gives us a daily cross to develop a life of faith based on what He has done. He wants to see us grow daily as any parent would like to have a child grow. He wants us to grow and live in faith.

Jesus made a clear point in communion with His disciples. Communion was designed to be conducted by His followers to remember Him. The daily cross involves bringing to daily action fellowship with Christ; therefore, it is a daily and continuous communion with Christ in our thought life. We should be able to sense when our thinking goes out of fellowship with Christ for a second. This awareness is vital because our thought life or imagination can become our actions and lifestyles.

Satan comes in both our small thoughts and our daydreams, and if these thoughts are not dealt with upon arrival, they will stay, and more of the same thoughts will keep showing up at various intervals to build a foundation on original thought allowed. As ungodly thoughts are allowed to linger, they will grow in number and continue to expand.

God has made a provision for us to deal with thoughts and machinations that are not in line with the Word of God. Every thought that goes against the knowledge of God should be cast down immediately. Evil thoughts will come to interrupt our communion with God. We need to open our mouths and say, "Satan, I cast you down or out in the name of Jesus. Your power is void in the name of Jesus" (2 Corinthians 10:5).

Daily communion with Christ comes from within and is demonstrated through our thoughts, senses, and actions. If we have to set alarms for this daily communion until we enter into it naturally, then that is what we must do. The Spirit is always willing, but the flesh is weak (Matthew 26:41). Christ has done his part, and we need to do whatever we can to desire and walk in communion with God, for faith without works is dead (James 2:14-26).

Daily communion involves praying in the name of Jesus, pleading the power of the blood of Christ; allowing the Lord Jesus Christ to rebuke Satan in areas he attempts to operate; wrestling in spiritual warfare by faith in Christ; repentance and allowing Jesus to deal with sin in your life, and allowing Jesus to deliver you from every temptation daily. Depending on Jesus daily is the key here, along with doing the best you can on your part.

Daily communion involves meditation, prayer, hearing the Word, praise, worship, and sometimes, fasting. Whatever it takes, that is what we must do.

Remembrance means to bring the past to the present. Jesus wants communion with Him to be always present in our lives. He wants a new covenant in which we are to be present and active daily. The body of Christ is bread for dead sinners to come back to life, and it is bread for sinners to gain and maintain life. Communion is needed for saints to stay alive. Communion helps our participation in the body of Christ as Christ Himself would. Being in communion with Christ should reflect how we treat others, especially within the body of Christ. Communion is a life of exchange between Christ and us. Christ is living in us, and we are living in Christ.

When it comes to daily communion, we must be aware of Satan's wiles to steal our time and distract us away from the time we should reserve for communion with God.

In today's world, we all know that electronic devices are a major distraction to our communion with God. We must be conscious of any distraction, not just technology related, that interrupts our daily communion with God. In the modern world, it is too easy for us to forget what really matters because of too many interruptions and distractions. Sometimes, we can even be deceived by church programs, forgetting that our communion with Christ is of most importance.

We saw this with the two sisters Martha and Mary. Mary chose to have communion with God, while Martha was distracted by many things (Luke 10:38-42). Martha was certainly distracted with ongoing activities to the point of blindness to the value of communion with Christ, but Mary valued such communion more than her usual activities. Sometimes, we've got to understand the value of communion with Christ and allow our daily activities to be interrupted by Christ. Mary understood that communion comes before service. Although Martha thought she was serving Jesus through activities, Jesus commended her sister Mary for actually allowing her business to be interrupted for communion with Christ.

Communion with Christ should come before ministry with and for Christ. Communion involves learning and hearing from Jesus. After the resurrection, Jesus had communion with the disciples through the Holy Ghost. He communed with them from within. He gave them exactly what they will say when they needed to speak (Acts 2:4, John 16:13).

Communion through the Word of God is also important. We need to get in the habit of speaking the word of God constantly because faith comes by the influence of the Word on our lives. The bread representing the body of Christ in communion also represents the Word of God. The Word is our daily bread that we should live by if we are in covenant with God through His blood.

Sometimes, daily communion involves the practice of having Christ on our minds all the time. We can pray quietly in our hearts and minds as we go about our daily business. We can be in the presence of God in whatever we do. Everyone does not need to know that we may be in their company but have communion with Christ going on within us.

Communing with Christ all the time develops faith in what He has finished. Through the finished work of Christ on the cross, the Holy Spirit was sent to help us in our daily living. Communion with Christ helps us become sensitive to the daily prompts of the Holy Spirit. The Holy Spirit translates this everyday consciousness of the daily cross to our physical senses. As we develop this consciousness, we will begin to notice the prompts of the Holy Spirit. We will know when the Holy Spirit prompts us to turn our eyes from inappropriate images. We will see when the Holy Spirit prompts us to stay away from specific actions and places. We will hear what the Spirit speaks and speak what the Spirit says. This is important as we become sensitive to the natural impulses towards sin. Practicing communion with God by talking to Jesus as you would to people you see in reality comes with time. The practicing of communion is beneficial to our Christian walk. If we are disciplined enough with the practice without interruption, we will grow in several ways, and such growth will help us respond better to challenges and issues of this present time.

Exercising the Presence of God through the Holy Spirit

The Holy Spirit is a Watchman for our souls. The Holy Spirit alerts us each time the devil attempts to influence us. The Holy Spirit sends an alarm through our spirits on each attempt the devil makes to contact us. Sometimes, the panic is strong and powerful enough to trigger the physical body as self puts up a fight to resist.

For example, if the Holy Spirit warns you to tell the truth, and you want to lie, you will feel this great warfare that will change your peaceful nature of the cross. The Holy Spirit will pull the trigger each time a child of God acts outside of Biblical boundaries. God sets limits for the protection of your soul.

To appropriately respond to the alarm, we must deal with self. Dealing with self is personal in this case because one is responsible for deciding and choosing what goes in and out of one's life with the help of the Spirit.

Practicing the daily cross through communion with Christ is beneficial in the Christian walk. It is through communion with God that we are given God's will through Jesus Christ daily. Without communion with Christ, we will not know the daily cross.

Pages are not enough to overemphasize the importance of the practice of the daily communion in taking the daily cross. From Abraham, then Isaac, to Jacob, we saw how they valued communion. They allowed their activities to be interrupted in order to spend time with God. Abraham, Isaac, and Jacob all built altars wherever they went. Isaac meditated daily. Anna and Simeon communed with God through fasting and prayer until they saw the Messiah. Jesus, in in the flesh, took time out to commune with the Father. We are not exempted from taking time to commune with the father.

Communion is the essence of our Christian life.

ABOUT THE AUTHOR

It is not about the author, but about the cross of Jesus Christ. Therefore, this excerpt is only for informational purposes for the curious.

The author desires readers to view him as one who was once bound and controlled by the prince and power of the air and walked according to the course of this world, the spirit that now worketh in the children of disobedience (Ephesians 2:2). He was unfit and unworthy to take the cross and undeserving of grace, but the grace of God, which carries salvation to all, still appeared to him through a God who so dearly loves him and gave His only Son for him (John 3:16). His unworthiness of the grace which has been so freely poured on him makes him see himself as the least among the saints to whom this grace was given to preach the unsearchable riches of Christ (Ephesians 3:8). His greatest accomplishment is the acceptance of this unmerited grace through repentance.

The author lives in western Maryland with his family and is a citizen of God's kingdom. His current spiritual address within the body of Christ is Virginia Avenue Church of God, where he leads the prayer ministry.

Although the author is ordained and holds degrees in Biblical Studies, Paralegal Studies, Cybersecurity, and multiple certifications, he has no glory in such accomplishments. He counts all things as dung for the sake of the humble cross of Christ, not to be boastful of any status (Philippians 3:8). The author prays not to be in the sad, empty state of placing much emphasis on things of vanity as human status and accomplishments, as stated by the preacher: "Vanity of vanities, saith the Preacher, vanity of vanities; all is vanity" (Ecclesiastes 1:2). He is humbled to continually pursue the cross.

He is the organizer of CLEAN PAGE fellowship, an association of individuals who believe in pursuing what God wants and encouraging others to do likewise. Also, he offers free cross life leadership training for startup churches and young people free of charge.

Please visit www.johngenda.org for further information.